THE SECRETS OF THE SELF
(ASRAR-I KHUDI)

THE SECRETS OF THE SELF

(ASRAR-I KHUDI)

A PHILOSOPHICAL POEM

BY

SHEIKH MUHAMMADIQBAL

OF LAHORE

TRANSLATED FROM THE ORIGINAL PERSIAN
WITH INTRODUCTON AND NOTES BY

REYNOLD A. NICHOLSON, LITT. D., LL.D.

LECTURER ON PERSIAN IN THE UNIVERSITY OF CAMBRIDGE

KALPAZ

ISBN: 978-93-5128-799-5(HB)

First Published in 1920
Indian Reprint in 2017

Published by

Kalpaz Publications
C-30, Satyawati Nagar,
Delhi – 110052
E-mail: kalpaz@hotmail.com
Website: kalpazpublications.com
Ph.: +91-9212142040

Cataloging in Publication Data—DK
Courtesy: D.K. Agencies (P) Ltd. <docinfo@dkagencies.com>

Iqbal, Muhammad, *Sir,* 1877-1938, **author.**
[Asra˜r-i khu˜di˜. English]
The secrets of the self : a philosophical poem = Asrar-i khudiì / by Sheikh Muhammad Iqbal of Lahore ; translated from the original Persian with introduction and notes by Reynold A. Nicholson (LITT. D., LL.D.).
pages cm
"First published in 1920"—Title page verso.
ISBN 9789351287995

1. Islamic poetry, Persian—Translations into English. I. Nicholson, Reynold Alleyne, 1868-1945, translator. II. Title. III. Title: Asrar-i khudiì.

PK6561.I5A87 2017 DDC 891.5513 23

CONTENTS

INTRODUCTION

THE *Asrár-i Khudí* was first published at Lahore in 1915. I read it soon afterwards and thought so highly of it that I wrote to Iqbal, whom I had the pleasure of meeting at Cambridge some fifteen years ago, asking leave to prepare an English translation. My proposal was cordially accepted, but in the meantime I found other work to do, which caused the translation to be laid aside until last year. Before submitting it to the reader, a few remarks are necessary concerning the poem and its author.[1]

[1] The present translation follows the text of the second edition.

Iqbal is an Indian Moslem. During his stay in the West he studied modern philosophy, in which subject he holds degrees from the Universities of Cambridge and Munich. His dissertation on the development of metaphysics in Persia — an illuminating sketch — appeared as a book in 1908. Since then he has developed a philosophy of his own, on which I am able to give some extremely interesting notes communicated by himself. Of this, however, the *Asrár-i Khudí* gives no systematic account, though it puts his ideas in a popular and attractive form. While the Hindu philosophers, in explaining the doctrine of the unity of being, addressed themselves to the head, Iqbal, like the Persian poets who teach the same doctrine, takes a more dangerous course and aims at the heart. He is no mean poet, and his verse can rouse or persuade even if his logic fail to convince. His message is not for the Mohammedans of India alone, but for Moslems everywhere: accordingly he writes in Persian instead of Hindustani —a happy choice, for amongst educated Moslems there are many familiar with Persian literature, while the Persian language is singularly well adapted to express philosophical ideas in a style at once elevated and charming.

Iqbal comes forward as an apostle, if not to his own age, then to posterity—

> "I have no need of the ear of To-day,
> I am the voice of the poet of To-morrow"—

and after Persian fashion he invokes the Saki to fill his cup with wine and pour moonbeams into the dark night of his thought,

> "That I may lead home the wanderer,
> And imbue the idle looker-on with restless impatience,
> And advance hotly on a new quest,
> And become known as the champion of a new spirit."

Let us begin at the end. What is the far-off goal on which his eyes are fixed? The answer to that question will discover his true character, and we shall be less likely to stumble on the way if we see whither we are going. Iqbal has drunk deep of European literature, his philosophy owes much to Nietzsche and Bergson, and his poetry often reminds us of Shelley; yet he thinks and feels as a Moslem, and just for this reason his influence may be great. He is a religious enthusiast, inspired by the vision of a New Mecca, a world-wide, theocratic, Utopian state in which all Moslems, no longer divided by the barriers of race and country, shall be one. He will have nothing to do with nationalism and imperialism. These, he says, "rob us of Paradise": they make us strangers to each other, destroy feelings of brotherhood, and sow the bitter seed of war. He dreams of a world ruled by religion, not by politics, and condemns Machiavelli, that "worshipper of false gods," who has blinded so many. It must be observed that when he speaks of religion he always means Islam. Non-Moslems are simply unbelievers, and (in theory, at any rate) the *Jihád* is justifiable, provided that it is waged "for God's sake alone." A free and independent Moslem fraternity, having the Ka'ba as its centre and knit together by love of Allah and devotion to the Prophet—such is Iqbal's ideal. In the *Asrár-i Khudí* and the *Rumúz-i Békhudí* he preaches it with a burning sincerity which we cannot but admire, and at the same time points out how it may be attained. The former poem deals with the life of the individual Moslem, the latter with the life of the Islamic community.

The cry "Back to the Koran! Back

to Mohammed!" has been heard before, and the responses have hitherto been somewhat discouraging. But on this occasion it is allied with the revolutionary force of Western philosophy, which Iqbal hopes and believes will vitalise the movement and ensure its triumph. He sees that Hindu intellectualism and Islamic pantheism have destroyed the capacity for action, based on scientific observation and interpretation of phenomena, which distinguishes the Western peoples "and especially the English." Now, this capacity depends ultimately on the conviction that *khudí* (selfhood, individuality, personality) is real and is not merely an illusion of the mind. Iqbal, therefore, throws himself with all his might against idealistic philosophers and pseudo-mystical poets, the authors, in his opinion, of the decay prevailing in Islam, and argues that only by self-affirmation, self-expression, and self-development can the Moslems once more become strong and free. He appeals from the alluring raptures of Hafiz to the moral fervour of Jalál-u'ddín Rúmí, from an Islam sunk in Platonic contemplation to the fresh and vigorous monotheism which inspired Mohammed and brought Islam into existence.[1] Here, perhaps, I should guard against a possible misunderstanding. Iqbal's philosophy is religious, but he does not treat philosophy as the handmaid of religion. Holding that the full development of the individual presupposes a society, he finds the ideal society in what he considers to be the Prophet's conception of Islam. Every Moslem, in striving to make himself a

[1] His criticism of Hafiz called forth angry protests from Súfí circles in which Hafiz is venerated as a master-hierophant. Iqbal made no recantation, but since the passage had served its purpose and was offensive to many, he cancelled it in the second edition of the poem. It is omitted in my translation.

more perfect individual, is helping to establish the Islamic kingdom of God upon earth.[1]

The *Asrár-i Khudí* is composed in the metre and modelled on the style of the famous *Masnaví.* In the prologue Iqbal relates how Jalálu'ddín Rúmí, who is to him almost what Virgil was to Dante, appeared in a vision and bade him arise and sing. Much as he dislikes the type of Súfism exhibited by Hafiz, he pays homage to the pure and profound genius of Jalálu'ddín, though he rejects the doctrine of self-abandonment taught by the great Persian

[1] The principles of Islam, regarded as the ideal society, are set forth in the author's second poem, the *Rumúz-i Békhudí* or "Mysteries of Selflessness." He explains the title by pointing out that the individual who loses himself in the community reflects both the past and the future as in a mirror, so that he transcends mortality and enters into the life of Islam, which is infinite and everlasting. Among the topics discussed are the origin of society, the divine guidance of man through the prophets, the formation of collective life-centres, and the value of History as a factor in maintaining the sense of personal identity in a people.

mystic and does not accompany him in his pantheistic flights.

To European readers the *Asrár-i Khudí* presents certain obscurities which no translation can entirely remove. These lie partly in the form and would not be felt, as a rule, by any one conversant with Persian poetry. Often, however, the ideas themselves, being associated with peculiarly Oriental ways of thinking, are hard for our minds to follow. I am not sure that I have always grasped the meaning or rendered it correctly; but I hope that such errors are few, thanks to the assistance so kindly given me by my friend Muhammad Shafi, now Professor of Arabic at Lahore, with whom I read the poem and discussed many points of difficulty. Other questions of a more fundamental character have been solved for me by the author himself. At my request he drew up a statement of his philosophical views on the problems touched and suggested in the book. I will give it in his own words as nearly as possible. It is not, of course, a complete statement, and was written, as he says, "in a great hurry," but apart from its power and originality it elucidates the poetical argument far better than any explanation that could have been offered by me.

"1. The Philosophical Basis of the *Asrár-i Khudí*

"'That experience should take place in finite centres and should wear the form of finite this-ness is in the end inexplicable.' These are the words of Prof. Bradley. But starting with these inexplicable centres of experience, he ends in a unity which he calls Absolute and in which the finite centres lose their finiteness and distinctness. According to him, therefore, the finite centre is only an appearance. The test of reality, in his opinion, is all-inclusiveness; and since all finiteness is 'infected with relativity,' it follows that the latter is a mere illusion. To my mind, this inexplicable finite centre of experience is the fundamental fact of the universe. All life is individual; there is no such thing as universal life. God himself is an individual: He is the most unique individual.[1] The universe, as Dr. McTaggart says, is an association of individuals; but we must add that the orderliness and adjustment which we find in this association is not eternally achieved and complete in itself. It is the result of instinctive or conscious effort. We are gradually travelling from chaos to cosmos and are helpers in this achievement. Nor are the members of the association fixed; new members are ever coming to birth to

[1] This view was held by the orthodox Imám Ahmad ibn Hanbal in its extreme (anthropomorphic) form.

co-operate in the great task. Thus the universe is not a completed act: it is still in the course of formation. There can be no complete truth about the universe, for the universe has not yet become 'whole.' The process of creation is still going on, and man too takes his share in it, inasmuch as he helps to bring order into at least a portion of the chaos. The Koran indicates the possibility of other creators than God.[1]

"Obviously, this view of man and the universe is opposed to that of the English Neo-Hegelians as well as to all forms of pantheistic Súfism which regard absorption in a universal life or soul as the final aim and salvation of man.[2] The moral and religious ideal of man is not self-negation but self-affirmation, and he attains to this ideal

[1] Kor. ch. 23, v. 14: "Blessed is God, the best of those who create."

[2] Cf. his note on "Islam and Mysticism" (*The New Era*, 1916, p. 250).

by becoming more and more individual, more and more unique. The Prophet said, '*Takhallaqú bi-akhláq Allah,*' 'Create in yourselves the attributes of God.' Thus man becomes unique by becoming more and more like the most unique Individual. What then is life? It is individual: its highest form, so far, is the Ego (*Khudí*) in which the individual becomes a self-contained exclusive centre. Physically as well as spiritually man is a self-contained centre, but he is not yet a complete individual. The greater his distance from God, the less his individuality. He who comes nearest to God is the completest person. Not that he is finally absorbed in God. On the contrary, he absorbs God into himself.[1]

[1] Here Iqbal adds: "Mauláná Rúmí has very beautifully expressed this idea. The Prophet, when a little boy, was once lost in the desert. His nurse Halíma was almost beside herself with grief, but while roaming the desert in search of the boy she heard a voice saying:

The true person not only absorbs the world of matter; by mastering it he absorbs God Himself into his Ego. Life is a forward assimilative movement. It removes all obstructions in its march by assimilating them. Its essence is the continual creation of desires and ideals, and for the purpose of its preservation and expansion it has invented or developed out of itself certain instruments, *e.g.* senses, intellect, etc., which help it to assimilate obstructions.[1] The greatest obstacle in the way of life is matter, Nature; yet Nature is not evil, since it enables the inner powers of life to unfold themselves.

> 'Do not grieve, he will not be lost to thee;
> Nay, the whole world will be lost in him.'

The true individual cannot be lost in the world; it is the world that is lost in him. I go a step further and say, prefixing a new half-verse to a hemistich of Rúmí (Transl. l. 1325):

> In his will that which God wills becomes lost:
> 'How shall a man believe this saying?'"

[1] Transl. l. 289 foll.

"The Ego attains to freedom by the removal of all obstructions in its way. It is partly free, partly determined,[1] and reaches fuller freedom by approaching the Individual who is most free—God. In one word, life is an endeavour for freedom.

"2. The Ego and Continuation of Personality

"In man the centre of life becomes an Ego or Person. Personality is a state of tension and can continue only if that state is maintained. If the state of tension is not maintained, relaxation will ensue. Since personality, or the state of tension, is the most valuable achievement of man, he should see that he does not revert to a state of relaxation. That which tends to maintain

[1] According to the Tradition, "The true Faith is between predestination and freewill."

the state of tension tends to make us immortal. Thus the idea of personality gives us a standard of value: it settles the problem of good and evil. That which fortifies personality is good, that which weakens it is bad. Art,[1] religion, and ethics[2] must be judged from the standpoint of personality. My criticism of Plato[3] is directed against those philosophical systems which hold up death rather than life as their ideal—systems which ignore the greatest obstruction to life, namely, matter, and

[1] Transl. l. 673 foll. In a note on "Our Prophet's criticism of contemporary Arabian poetry" (*The New Era*, 1916, p. 251) Iqbal writes: "The ultimate end of all human activity is Life—glorious, powerful, exuberant. All human art must be subordinated to this final purpose, and the value of everything must be determined in reference to its life-yielding capacity. The highest art is that which awakens our dormant will-force and nerves us to face the trials of life manfully. All that brings drowsiness and makes us shut our eyes to Reality around, on the mastery of which alone Life depends, is a message of decay and death. There should be no opium-eating in Art. The dogma of Art for the sake of Art is a clever invention of decadence to cheat us out of life and power."

[2] *Ibid.* l. 537 foll.

[3] *Ibid.* l. 631 foll.

teach us to run away from it instead of absorbing it.

"As in connexion with the question of the freedom of the Ego we have to face the problem of matter, similarly in connexion with its immortality we have to face the problem of time.[1] Bergson has taught us that time is not an infinite line (in the spatial sense of the word 'line') through which we must pass whether we wish it or not. This idea of time is adulterated. Pure time has no length. Personal immortality is an aspiration: you can have it if you make an effort to achieve it. It depends on our adopting in this life modes of thought and activity which tend to maintain the state of tension. Buddhism, Persian Súfism, and allied forms of ethics will not serve our purpose. But they are not wholly useless, because after periods of great activity we need

[1] *Ibid.* l. 1531 foll.

opiates, narcotics, for some time. These forms of thought and action are like nights in the days of life. Thus, if our activity is directed towards the maintenance of a state of tension, the shock of death is not likely to affect it. After death there may be an interval of relaxation, as the Koran speaks of a *barzakh*, or intermediate state, which lasts until the Day of Resurrection.[1] Only those Egos will survive this state of relaxation who have taken good care during the present life. Although life abhors repetition in its evolution, yet on Bergson's principles the resurrection of the body too, as Wildon Carr says, is quite possible. By breaking up time into moments we spatialise it and then find difficulty in getting over it. The true nature of time is reached when we look into our deeper self.[2] Real time is life itself, which can preserve itself

[1] Kor. ch. 23, v. 102. [2] Transl. l. 1549 foll.

by maintaining that particular state of tension (personality) which it has so far achieved. We are subject to time so long as we look upon time as something spatial. Spatialised time is a fetter which life has forged for itself in order to assimilate the present environment. In reality we are timeless, and it is possible to realise our timelessness even in this life. This revelation, however, can be momentary only.

"3. The Education of the Ego

"The Ego is fortified by love (*'ishq*).[1] This word is used in a very wide sense and means the desire to assimilate, to absorb. Its highest form is the creation of values and ideals and the endeavour to realise them. Love individualises the lover as well as the beloved. The effort to realise the most unique individuality individualises the seeker

[1] *Ibid.* l. 323 foll.

and implies the individuality of the sought, for nothing else would satisfy the nature of the seeker. As love fortifies the Ego, asking (*su'ál*) weakens it.[1] All that is achieved without personal effort comes under *su'ál*. The son of a rich man who inherits his father's wealth is an 'asker' (beggar); so is every one who thinks the thoughts of others. Thus, in order to fortify the Ego we should cultivate love, *i.e.* the power of assimilative action, and avoid all forms of 'asking,' *i.e.* inaction. The lesson of assimilative action is given by the life of the Prophet, at least to a Mohammedan.

"In another part of the poem[2] I have hinted at the general principles of Moslem ethics and have tried to reveal their meaning in connexion with the idea of personality. The Ego in its movement towards uniqueness has to pass through three stages:

[1] *Ibid.* l. 435 foll. [2] *Ibid.* l. 815 foll.

(*a*) Obedience to the Law.

(*b*) Self-control, which is the highest form of self-consciousness or Ego-hood.[1]

(*c*) Divine vicegerency.[2]

"This (divine vicegerency, *niyábat-i iláhí*) is the third and last stage of human development on earth. The *ná'ib* (vicegerent) is the vicegerent of God on earth. He is the completest Ego, the goal of humanity,[3] the acme of life both in mind and body; in him the discord of our mental life becomes a harmony. The highest power is united in him with the highest knowledge. In his life, thought and action, instinct and reason, become one. He is the last fruit of the tree of humanity, and all the trials of a painful evolution

[1] *Ibid.* l. 849 foll. [2] *Ibid.* l. 893 foll.

[3] Man already possesses the germ of vicegerency, as God says in the Koran (ch. 2, v. 28): "Lo, I will appoint a *khalífa* (vicegerent) on the earth." Cf. Transl. l. 434.

are justified because he is to come at the end. He is the real ruler of mankind; his kingdom is the kingdom of God on earth. Out of the richness of his nature he lavishes the wealth of life on others, and brings them nearer and nearer to himself. The more we advance in evolution, the nearer we get to him. In approaching him we are raising ourselves in the scale of life. The development of humanity both in mind and body is a condition precedent to his birth. For the present he is a mere ideal; but the evolution of humanity is tending towards the production of an ideal race of more or less unique individuals who will become his fitting parents. Thus the Kingdom of God on earth means the democracy of more or less unique individuals, presided over by the most unique individual possible on this earth. Nietzsche had a glimpse of this ideal race, but his atheism and aristocratic prejudices marred his whole conception."[1]

Every one, I suppose, will acknowledge that the substance of the *Asrár-i Khudí* is striking enough to command attention. In the poem, naturally, this philosophy presents itself under a different aspect. Its audacity of thought and phrase is less apparent, its logical brilliancy dissolves in the glow of feeling and imagination, and it wins the heart before taking possession of the

[1] Writing of "Muslim Democracy" in *The New Era*, 1916, p. 251, Iqbal says: "The Democracy of Europe—overshadowed by socialistic agitation and anarchical fear—originated mainly in the economic regeneration of European societies. Nietzsche, however, abhors this 'rule of the herd' and, hopeless of the plebeian, he bases all higher culture on the cultivation and growth of an Aristocracy of Supermen. But is the plebeian so absolutely hopeless? The Democracy of Islam did not grow out of the extension of economic opportunity; it is a spiritual principle based on the assumption that every human being is a centre of latent power, the possibilities of which can be developed by cultivating a certain type of character. Out of the plebeian material Islam has formed men of the noblest type of life and power. Is not, then, the Democracy of early Islam an experimental refutation of the ideas of Nietzsche?"

mind. The artistic quality of the poem is remarkable when we consider that its language is not the author's own. I have done my best to preserve as much of this as a literal prose translation would allow. Many passages of the original are poetry of the kind that, once read, is not easily forgotten, *e.g.* the description of the Ideal Man as a deliverer for whom the world is waiting, and the noble invocation which brings the book to an end. Like Jalálu'ddín Rúmí, Iqbal is fond of introducing fables and apologues to relieve the argument and illustrate his meaning with more force and point than would be possible otherwise.

On its first appearance the *Asrár-i Khudí* took by storm the younger generation of Indian Moslems. "Iqbal," wrote one of them, "has come amongst us as a Messiah and has stirred the dead with life." It remains to be seen in what direction the awakened ones will march. Will they be satisfied with a glorious but distant vision of the City of God, or will they adapt the new doctrine to other ends than those which its author has in view? Notwithstanding that he explicitly denounces the idea of nationalism, his admirers are already protesting that he does not mean what he says.

How far the influence of his work may ultimately go I will not attempt to prophesy. It has been said of him that "he is a man of his age and a man in advance of his age; he is also a man in disagreement with his age." We cannot regard his ideas as typical of any section of his co-religionists. They involve a radical change in the Moslem mind, and their real importance is not to be measured by the fact that such a change is unlikely to occur within a calculable time.

PROLOGUE

WHEN the world-illuming sun rushed upon Night like a brigand,
My weeping bedewed the face of the rose.
My tears washed away sleep from the eye of the narcissus,
My passion wakened the grass and made it grow.
The Gardener taught me to sing with power,
He sowed a verse and reaped a sword.
In the soil he planted only the seed of my tears
And wove my lament with the garden, as warp and woof.

Tho' I am but a mote, the radiant sun is mine:
Within my bosom are a hundred dawns.
My dust is brighter than Jamshíd's cup,[1]
It knows things that are yet unborn in the world.
My thought hunted down and slung from the saddle a deer
That has not yet leaped forth from the covert of non-existence.
Fair is my garden ere yet the leaves are green:
Full-blown roses are hidden in the skirt of my garment.
I struck dumb the musicians where they were gathered together,
I smote the heartstrings of all that heard me,
Because the lute of my genius hath a rare melody:
Even to comrades my song is strange.

[1] Jamshíd, one of the mythical Persian kings, is said to have possessed a marvellous cup in which the whole world was displayed to him.

I am born in the world as a new sun,
I have not learned the ways and fashions of the sky:
Not yet have the stars fled before my splendour,
Not yet is my quicksilver astir;
Untouched is the sea by my dancing rays,
Untouched are the mountains by my crimson hue.
The eye of existence is not familiar with me;
I rise trembling, afraid to show myself.
From the East my dawn arrived and routed Night,
A fresh dew settled on the rose of the world.
I am waiting for the votaries that rise at dawn:
Oh, happy they who shall worship my fire!
I have no need of the ear of To-day,
I am the voice of the poet of To-morrow.

My own age does not understand my
deep meanings,
My Joseph is not for this market.
I despair of my old companions,
My Sinai burns for sake of the Moses
who is coming.
Their sea is silent, like dew,
But my dew is storm-ridden, like the
ocean.
My song is of another world than theirs:
This bell calls other travellers to take
the road.
How many a poet after his death
Opened our eyes when his own were
closed,
And journeyed forth again from
nothingness
When roses blossomed o'er the earth of
his grave!
Albeit caravans have passed through
this desert,
They passed, as a camel steps, with
little sound.

But I am a lover: loud crying is my faith:
The clamour of Judgement Day is one of my minions.
My song exceeds the range of the chord,
Yet I do not fear that my lute will break.
'Twere better for the waterdrop not to know my torrent,
Whose fury should rather madden the sea.
No river will contain my Omán:[1]
My flood requires whole seas to hold it.
Unless the bud expand into a bed of roses,
It is unworthy of my spring-cloud's bounty.
Lightnings slumber within my soul,
I sweep over mountain and plain.
Wrestle with my sea, if thou art a plain;

[1] The Sea of Omán is a name given by the Arabs to the Persian Gulf.

Receive my lightning, if thou art a Sinai.
The Fountain of Life hath been given me to drink,
I have been made an adept of the mystery of Life.
The speck of dust was vitalised by my burning song:
It unfolded wings and became a firefly.
No one hath told the secret which I will tell
Or threaded a pearl of thought like mine.
Come, if thou would'st know the secret of everlasting life!
Come, if thou would'st win both earth and heaven!
The old Guru of the Sky taught me this lore,
I cannot hide it from my comrades.

O Saki! arise and pour wine into the cup,

Clear the vexation of Time from my heart!
The sparkling liquor that flows from Zemzem—[1]
Were it a beggar, a king would pay homage to it.
It makes thought more sober and wise,
It makes the keen eye keener,
It gives to a straw the weight of a mountain,
And to foxes the strength of lions.
It causes dust to soar to the Pleiades
And a drop of water swell to the breadth of the sea.
It turns silence into the din of Judgement Day,
It makes the foot of the partridge red with blood of the hawk.
Arise and pour pure wine into my cup,
Pour moonbeams into the dark night of my thought,

[1] The holy well at Mecca.

That I may lead home the wanderer
And imbue the idle looker-on with restless impatience;
And advance hotly on a new quest
And become known as the champion of a new spirit;
And be to people of insight as the pupil to the eye,
And sink into the ear of the world, like a voice;
And exalt the worth of Poesy
And sprinkle the dry herbs with my tears.
Inspired by the genius of the Master of Rúm,[1]
I rehearse the sealed book of secret lore.
His soul is the source of the flames,
I am but as the spark that gleams for a moment.

[1] Jalálu'ddín Rúmí, the greatest mystical poet of Persia (A.D. 1207–1273). Most of his life was passed at Iconium in Galatia, for which reason he is generally known as "Rúmí," *i.e.* "the Anatolian."

His burning candle consumed me, the moth;
His wine overwhelmed my goblet.
The Master of Rúm transmuted my earth to gold
And clothed my barren dust with beauty.
The grain of sand set forth from the desert,
That it might win the radiance of the sun.
I am a wave and I will come to rest in his sea,
That I may make the glistening pearl mine own.
I who am drunken with the wine of his song
Will draw life from the breath of his words.

'Twas night: my heart would fain lament,
The silence was filled with my cries to God.

I was complaining of the sorrows of the world
And bewailing the emptiness of my cup.
At last mine eye could endure no more,
Broken with fatigue it went to sleep.
There appeared the Master, formed in the mould of Truth,
Who wrote the Koran of Persia.[1]
He said, "O frenzied lover,
Take a draught of love's pure wine.
Strike the chords of thine heart and rouse a tumultuous strain,
Dash thine head against the cupping-glass and thine eye against the lancet!
Make thy laughter the source of a hundred sighs,
Make the hearts of men bleed with thy tears!
How long wilt thou be silent, like a bud?
Sell thy fragrance cheap, like the rose!

[1] This refers to the famous *Masnaví* of Jalálu'ddín Rúmí.

Tongue-tied, thou art in pain:
Cast thyself upon the fire, like rue![1]
Like the bell, break silence at last, and from every limb
Utter forth a lamentation!
Thou art fire: fill the world with thy glow!
Make others burn with thy burning!
Proclaim the secrets of the old wine-seller;[2]
Be thou a surge of wine, and the crystal cup thy robe!
Shatter the mirror of fear,
Break the bottles in the bazaar!
Like the reed-flute, bring a message from the reeds;
Give to Majnún a message from Lailá![3]
Create a new style for thy song,
Enrich the feast with thy piercing strains!

[1] Rue-seed, which is burned for the purpose of fumigation, crackles in the fire.
[2] "Wine" signifies the mysteries of divine love.
[3] Majnún is the Orlando Furioso of Arabia.

Up, and re-inspire every living soul!
Say 'Arise!' and by that word quicken the living!
Up, and set thy feet on another path;
Put aside the passionate melancholy of old!
Become familiar with the delight of singing;
O bell of the caravan, awake!"

At these words my bosom was enkindled
And swelled with emotion like the flute;
I rose like music from the string
To prepare a Paradise for the ear.
I unveiled the mystery of the Self
And disclosed its wondrous secret.

My being was as an unfinished statue,
Uncomely, worthless, good for nothing.
Love chiselled me: I became a man
And gained knowledge of the nature of the universe.

I have seen the movement of the sinews of the sky,
And the blood coursing in the veins of the moon.
Many a night I wept for Man's sake
That I might tear the veil from Life's mysteries,
And extract the secret of Life's constitution
From the laboratory of phenomena.
I who give beauty to this night, like the moon,
Am as dust in devotion to the pure Faith (Islam)—
A Faith renowned in hill and dale,
Which kindles in men's hearts a flame of undying song:
It sowed an atom and reaped a sun,
It harvested a hundred poets like Rúmí and Attár.
I am a sigh: I will mount to the heavens;
I am a breath, yet am I sprung of fire.

Driven onward by high thoughts, my pen
Cast abroad the secret of this veil,
That the drop may become co-equal with the sea
And the grain of sand grow into a Sahara.
Poetising is not the aim of this *masnaví*,
Beauty-worshipping and love-making is not its aim.
I am of India: Persian is not my native tongue;
I am like the crescent moon: my cup is not full.
Do not seek from me charm of style in exposition,
Do not seek from me Khánsár and Isfahan.[1]
Although the language of Hind is sweet as sugar,
Yet sweeter is the fashion of Persian speech.

[1] Khánsár, which lies about a hundred miles north-west of Isfahan, was the birth-place of several Persian poets.

My mind was enchanted by its loveliness,
My pen became as a twig of the Burning Bush.
Because of the loftiness of my thoughts,
Persian alone is suitable to them.
O Reader, do not find fault with the wine-cup,
But consider attentively the taste of the wine.

I

Showing that the system of the universe originates in the Self, and that the continuation of the life of all individuals depends on strengthening the Self.

THE form of existence is an effect of the Self,
Whatsoever thou seest is a secret of the Self.
When the Self awoke to consciousness,
It revealed the universe of Thought.
A hundred worlds are hidden in its essence:
Self-affirmation brings Not-self to light.
By the Self the seed of hostility is sown in the world:
It imagines itself to be other than itself.

It makes from itself the forms of others
In order to multiply the pleasure of strife.
It is slaying by the strength of its arm
That it may become conscious of its own strength.
Its self-deceptions are the essence of Life;
Like the rose, it lives by bathing itself in blood.
For the sake of a single rose it destroys a hundred rose-gardens
And makes a hundred lamentations in quest of a single melody.
For one sky it produces a hundred new moons,
And for one word a hundred discourses.
The excuse for this wastefulness and cruelty
Is the shaping and perfecting of spiritual beauty.

The loveliness of Shírín justifies the anguish of Farhád,[1]
The fragrant navel justifies a hundred musk-deer.
'Tis the fate of moths to consume in flame:
The suffering of moths is justified by the candle.
The pencil of the Self limned a hundred to-days
In order to achieve the dawn of a single morrow.
Its flames burned a hundred Abrahams[2]
That the lamp of one Mohammed might be lighted.
Subject, object, means, and causes—
They all exist for the purpose of action.

[1] Shírín was loved by the Persian emperor Khusrau Parwíz. Farhád fell in love with her and cast himself down a precipice on hearing a false rumour of her death.

[2] Abraham is said to have been cast on a burning pile by order of Nimrod and miraculously preserved from harm.

The Self rises, kindles, falls, glows, breathes,
Burns, shines, walks, and flies.
The spaciousness of Time is its arena,
Heaven is a billow of the dust on its road.
From its rose-planting the world abounds in roses;
Night is born of its sleep, day springs from its waking.
It divided its flame into sparks
And taught the understanding to worship particulars.
It dissolved itself and created the atoms,
It was scattered for a little while and created the sands.
Then it wearied of dispersion
And by re-uniting itself it became the mountains.
'Tis the nature of the Self to manifest itself:
In every atom slumbers the might of the Self.

Power that is unexpressed and inert
Chains the faculties which lead to action.
Inasmuch as the life of the universe comes from the strength of the Self,
Life is in proportion to this strength.
When a drop of water gets the Self's lesson by heart,
It makes its worthless existence a pearl.
Wine is formless because its self is weak;
It receives a form by favour of the cup.
Although the cup of wine assumes a form,
It is indebted to us for its motion.
When the mountain loses its self, it turns into sands
And complains that the sea surges over it;
But the wave, so long as it remains a wave in the sea's bosom,
Makes itself a rider on the sea's back.

Light has been a beggar since the eye first rolled
And moved to and fro in search of beauty;
But forasmuch as the grass found a means of growth in its self,
Its aspiration clove the breast of the garden.
The candle too concatenated itself
And built itself out of atoms;
Then it made a practice of melting itself away and fled from its self
Until at last it trickled down from its own eye, like tears.
If the bezel had been more self-secure by nature,
It would not have suffered wounds,
But since it derives its value from the superscription,
Its shoulder is galled by the burden of another's name.
Because the earth is firmly based on self-existence,

The captive moon goes round it perpetually.
The being of the sun is stronger than that of the earth:
Therefore is the earth bewitched by the sun's eye.
The glory of the plane fixes our gaze,
The mountains are enriched by its majesty:
Its raiment is woven of fire,
Its origin is one self-assertive seed.
When Life gathers strength from the Self,
The river of Life expands into an ocean.

II

Showing that the life of the Self comes from forming desires and bringing them to birth.

LIFE is preserved by purpose:
Because of the goal its caravan-bell tinkles.
Life is latent in seeking,
Its origin is hidden in desire.
Keep desire alive in thy heart,
Lest thy little dust become a tomb.
Desire is the soul of this world of hue and scent,
The nature of every thing is faithful to desire.
Desire sets the heart dancing in the breast,

And by its glow the breast is made bright as a mirror.
It gives to earth the power of soaring,
It is a Khizr to the Moses of perception.[1]
From the flame of desire the heart takes life,
And when it takes life, all dies that is not true.
When it refrains from forming wishes,
Its pinion breaks and it cannot soar.
Desire is an emotion of the Self:
It is a restless wave of the Self's sea.
Desire is a noose for hunting ideals,
A binder of the book of deeds.
Negation of desire is death to the living,
Even as absence of burning extinguishes the flame.
What is the source of our wakeful eye?
Our delight in seeing hath taken visible shape.

[1] Cf. Koran, ch. 18, vv. 64-80. Khizr represents the mystic seer whose actions are misjudged by persons of less insight.

The partridge's leg is derived from the elegance of its gait,
The nightingale's beak from its endeavour to sing.
Away from the reed-bed, the reed became happy:
The music was released from its prison.[1]
Why does the mind strive after new discoveries and scale the heavens?
Knowest thou what works this miracle?
'Tis desire that enriches Life,
And the intellect is a child of its womb.
What are social organisation, customs, and laws?
What is the secret of the novelties of science?
A desire which broke through by its own strength
And burst forth from the heart and took shape.

[1] *I.e.* the reed was made into a flute.

Nose, hand, brain, eye, and ear,
Thought, imagination, feeling, memory, and understanding—
All these are weapons devised for self-preservation
By him that rides into the battle of Life.
The object of science and art is not knowledge,
The object of the garden is not the bud and the flower.
Science is an instrument for the preservation of Life,
Science is a means of establishing the Self.
Science and art are servants of Life,
Slaves born and bred in its house.
Rise, O thou who art strange to Life's mystery,
Rise intoxicated with the wine of an ideal!
If thou art an ideal, thou wilt shine as the dawn

And be to all else as a blazing fire.
If thou art an ideal, thou art higher
than Heaven—
Winning, captivating, enchanting men's
hearts;
A destroyer of ancient falsehood,
Fraught with turmoil, an embodiment
of the Last Day.
We live by forming ideals,
We glow with the sunbeams of desire!

III

Showing that the Self is strengthened by Love.[1]

THE luminous point whose name is the Self
Is the life-spark beneath our dust.
By Love it is made more lasting,
More living, more burning, more glowing.
From Love proceeds the radiance of its being
And the development of its unknown possibilities.
Its nature gathers fire from Love,
Love instructs it to illumine the world.

[1] For the sense which Iqbal attaches to the word "love," see the Introduction, p. xxv.

Love fears neither sword nor dagger,
Love is not born of water and air and earth.
Love makes peace and war in the world,
The Fountain of Life is Love's flashing sword.
The hardest rocks are shivered by Love's glance:
Love of God at last becomes wholly God.
Learn thou to love, and seek to be loved:
Seek an eye like Noah's, a heart like Job's!
Transmute thy handful of earth into gold,
Kiss the threshold of a Perfect Man![1]
Like Rúmí, light thy candle
And burn Rúm in the fire of Tabríz![2]

[1] A prophet or saint.

[2] See note on l. 95. Tabríz is an allusion to Shams-i Tabríz, the spiritual director of Jalálu'ddin Rúmí.

There is a beloved hidden within thine heart:
I will show him to thee, if thou hast eyes to see.
His lovers are fairer than the fair,
Sweeter and comelier and more beloved.
By love of him the heart is made strong
And earth rubs shoulders with the Pleiades.
The soil of Najd was quickened by his grace
And fell into a rapture and rose to the skies.[1]
In the Moslem's heart is the home of Mohammed,
All our glory is from the name of Mohammed.
Sinai is but an eddy of the dust of his house,
The sanctuary of the Ka'ba is his dwelling-place.

[1] Najd, the Highlands of Arabia, is celebrated in love-romance. I need only mention Lailá and Majnún.

Eternity is less than a moment of his time,
Eternity receives increase from his essence.
He slept on a mat of rushes,
But the crown of Chosroes was under his people's feet.
He chose the nightly solitude of Mount Hirá,
And he founded a state and laws and government.
He passed many a night with sleepless eyes
In order that the Moslems might sleep on the throne of Persia.
In the hour of battle, iron was melted by his sword;
In the hour of prayer, tears fell like rain from his eye.
When he was called to aid, his sword answered "Amen"
And extirpated the race of kings.
He instituted new laws in the world,

He brought the empires of antiquity to an end.
With the key of religion he opened the door of this world:
The womb of the world never bore his like.
In his sight high and low were one,
He sat with his slave at one table.
The daughter of the chieftain of Tai was taken prisoner in battle[1]
And brought into that exalted presence;
Her feet in chains, unveiled,
And her neck bowed with shame.
When the Prophet saw that the poor girl had no veil,
He covered her face with his own veil.
We are more naked than that lady of Tai,
We are unveiled before the nations of the world.

[1] Her father, Hátim of Tai, is proverbial in the East for his hospitality.

In him is our trust on the Day of Judgement,
And in this world too he is our protector.
Both his favour and his wrath are entirely a mercy:
That is a mercy to his friends and this to his foes.
He opened the gates of mercy to his enemies,
He gave to Mecca the message, "No blame shall be laid upon you."
We who know not the bonds of country
Resemble sight, which is one though it be the light of two eyes.
We belong to the Hijáz and China and Persia,
Yet we are the dew of one smiling dawn.
We are all under the spell of the eye of the cupbearer from Mecca,
We are united as wine and cup.

He burnt clean away distinctions of lineage,
His fire consumed this trash and rubble.
We are like a rose with many petals but with one perfume:
He is the soul of this society, and he is one.
We were the secret concealed in his heart:
He spake out fearlessly, and we were revealed.
The song of love for him fills my silent reed,
A hundred notes throb in my bosom.
How shall I tell what devotion he inspires?
A block of dry wood wept at parting from him.[1]
The Moslem's being is where he manifests his glory:
Many a Sinai springs from the dust on his path.

[1] The story of the pulpit that wept when Mohammed descended from it occurs, I think, in the *Masnavi*.

My image was created by his mirror,
My dawn rises from the sun of his breast.
My repose is a perpetual fever,
My evening hotter than the morning of Judgement Day:[1]
He is the April cloud and I his garden,
My vine is bedewed with his rain.
I sowed mine eye in the field of Love
And reaped a harvest of delight.
"The soil of Medina is sweeter than both worlds:
Oh, happy the town where dwells the Beloved!"[2]
I am lost in admiration of the style of Mullá Jámí:
His verse and prose are a remedy for my immaturity.
He has written poetry overflowing with beautiful ideas

1 When, according to Mohammedan belief, the sun will rise in the west.

2 A quotation from the *Masnaví*. The Prophet was buried at Medina.

And has threaded pearls in praise of the Master—
"Mohammed is the preface to the book of the universe:
All the world are slaves and he is the Master."
From the wine of Love spring many qualities:
Amongst the attributes of Love is blind devotion.
The saint of Bistám, who in devotion was unique,
Abstained from eating a water-melon.[1]
Be a lover constant in devotion to thy beloved,
That thou mayst cast thy noose and capture God.
Sojourn for a while on the Hirá of the heart,[2]

[1] Báyazíd of Bistám died in A.D. 875. He refused to eat a water-melon, saying he had no assurance that the Prophet had ever tasted that fruit.

[2] Mohammed used to retire to a cave on Mount Hirá, near Mecca, for the purpose of solitary meditation and other ascetic observances.

Abandon self and flee to God.
Strengthened by God, return to thy self
And break the heads of the Lát and Uzzá of sensuality.[1]
By the might of Love evoke an army,
Reveal thyself on the Fárán of Love,[2]
That the Lord of the Ka'ba may show thee favour
And interpret to thee the text, "Lo, I will appoint a vicegerent on the earth."[3]

[1] Lát and Uzzá were goddesses worshipped by the heathen Arabs.

[2] Fárán, name of a mountain in the neighbourhood of Mecca.

[3] Koran, ch. 2, v. 28. In these words, which were addressed to the angels, God foretold the creation of Adam.

IV

Showing that the Self is weakened by asking.

O THOU who hast gathered taxes from lions,
Thy need hath caused thee to become a fox in disposition.
Thy maladies are the result of indigence:
This disease is the source of thy pain.
It is robbing thine high thoughts of their dignity
And putting out the light of thy noble imagination.
Quaff rosy wine from the jar of existence!

Snatch thy money from the purse of Time!
Like Omar, come down from thy camel![1]
Beware of incurring obligations, beware!
How long wilt thou sue for office
And ride like children on a woman's back?
A nature that fixes its gaze on the sky
Becomes debased by receiving benefits.
By asking, poverty is made more abject;
By begging, the beggar is made poorer.
Asking disintegrates the Self
And deprives of illumination the Sinai-bush of the Self.
Do not scatter thy handful of dust;
Like the moon, scrape food from thine own side!
Albeit thou art poor and wretched

[1] The Caliph Omar was a man of simple habits and self-reliant character.

And overwhelmed by affliction,
Seek not thy daily bread from the bounty of another,
Seek not waves of water from the fountain of the sun,
Lest thou be put to shame before the Prophet
On the Day when every soul shall be stricken with fear.
The moon gets sustenance from the table of the sun
And bears the brand of his bounty on her heart.
Pray God for courage! Wrestle with Fortune!
Do not sully the honour of the pure religion!
He who swept the rubbish of idols out of the Ka'ba
Said that God loves a man that earns his living.
Woe to him that accepts bounty from another's table

And lets his neck be bent with benefits!
He hath consumed himself with the lightning of the favours bestowed on him,
He hath sold his honour for a paltry coin.
Happy the man who thirsting in the sun
Does not crave of Khizr a cup of water![1]
His brow is not moist with the shame of beggary;
He is a man still, not a piece of clay.
That noble youth walks under heaven
With his head erect like the pine.
Are his hands empty? The more is he master of himself.
Do his fortunes languish? The more alert is he.
The beggar's wallet is like a boat tossing in waves of fire;

[1] Khizr is supposed to have drunk of the Fountain of Life.

Sweet is a little dew gathered by one's own hand.
Be a man of honour, and like the bubble
Keep thy cup inverted even in the midst of the sea![1]

[1] The bubble is compared to an inverted cup, which of course receives nothing.

V

Showing that when the Self is strengthened by Love it gains dominion over the outward and inward forces of the universe.

WHEN the Self is made strong by Love
Its power rules the whole world.
The Heavenly Sage who adorned the sky with stars
Plucked these buds from the bough of the Self.
Its hand becomes God's hand,
The moon is split by its fingers.
It is the arbitrator in all the quarrels of the world,
Its command is obeyed by Darius and Jamshíd.

I will tell thee a story of Bú Ali,[1]
Whose name is renowned in India,
Him who sang of the ancient rose-garden
And discoursed to us about the lovely rose:
The air of his fluttering skirt
Made a Paradise of this fire-born country.
His young disciple went one day to the bazaar—
The wine of Bú Ali's discourse had turned his head.
The governor of the city was coming along on horseback,
His servant and staff-bearer rode beside him.
The forerunner shouted, "O senseless one,
Do not get in the way of the governor's escort!"

[1] Sheikh Sharafu'ddín of Pánípat, who is better known as Bú Ali Qalandar, was a great saint. He died about A.D. 1325.

But the dervish walked on with drooping head,
Sunk in the sea of his own thoughts.
The staff-bearer, drunken with pride,
Broke his staff on the head of the dervish,
Who stepped painfully out of the governor's way,
Sad and sorry, with a heavy heart.
He came to Bú Ali and complained
And released the tears from his eyes.
Like lightning that falls on mountains,
The Sheikh poured forth a fiery torrent of speech.
He let loose from his soul a strange fire,
He gave an order to his secretary:
"Take thy pen and write a letter
From a dervish to a sultan!
Say, 'Thy governor has broken my servant's head;
He has cast burning coals on his own life.

Arrest this wicked governor,
Or else I will bestow thy kingdom on another.'"
The letter of the saint who had access to God
Caused the monarch to tremble in every limb.
His body was filled with aches,
He grew as pale as the evening sun.
He sought out a handcuff for the governor
And entreated Bú Ali to pardon this offence.
Khusrau, the sweet-voiced eloquent poet,[1]
Whose harmonies flow from the creative mind
And whose genius hath the soft brilliance of moonlight,
Was chosen to be the king's ambassador.

[1] Amír Khusrau of Delhi, the most celebrated of the Persian poets of India.

When he entered Bú Ali's presence and played his lute,
His song melted the fakir's soul like glass.
One strain of poesy bought the grace
Of a majesty that was firm as a mountain.
Do not wound the hearts of dervishes,
Do not throw thyself into burning fire!

VI

A tale of which the moral is that negation of the Self is a doctrine invented by the subject races of mankind in order that by this means they may sap and weaken the character of their rulers.

HAST thou heard that in the time of old
The sheep dwelling in a certain pasture
So increased and multiplied
That they feared no enemy?
At last, from the malice of Fate,
Their breasts were smitten by a shaft of calamity.
The tigers sprang forth from the jungle
And rushed upon the sheepfold.

Conquest and dominion are signs of strength,
Victory is the manifestation of strength.
Those fierce tigers beat the drum of sovereignty,
They deprived the sheep of freedom.
Forasmuch as tigers must have their prey,
That meadow was crimsoned with the blood of the sheep.
One of the sheep which was clever and acute,
Old in years, cunning as a weather-beaten wolf,
Being grieved at the fate of his fellows
And sorely vexed by the violence of the tigers,
Made complaint of the course of Destiny
And sought by craft to restore his fortunes.
The weak man, in order to preserve himself,

Seeks devices from skilled intelligence.
In slavery, for the sake of repelling harm,
The power of scheming becomes quickened,
And when the madness of revenge gains hold,
The mind of the slave meditates rebellion.
"Ours is a hard knot," said this sheep to himself,
"The ocean of our griefs hath no shore.
By force we sheep cannot escape from the tiger:
Our legs are silver, his paws are steel.
'Tis not possible, however much one exhorts and counsels,
To create in a sheep the disposition of a wolf.
But to make the furious tiger a sheep—that is possible;
To make him unmindful of his nature—that is possible."

He became as a prophet inspired,
And began to preach to the blood-thirsty tigers.
He cried out, "O ye insolent liars,
Who wot not of a day of ill luck that shall continue for ever![1]
I am possessed of spiritual power,
I am an apostle sent by God for the tigers.
I come as a light for the eye that is dark,
I come to establish laws and give commandments.
Repent of your blameworthy deeds!
O plotters of evil, bethink yourselves of good!
Whoso is violent and strong is miserable:
Life's solidity depends on self-denial.
The spirit of the righteous is fed by fodder:
The vegetarian is pleasing unto God.

[1] These expressions are borrowed from the Koran.

The sharpness of your teeth brings disgrace upon you
And makes the eye of your perception blind.
Paradise is for the weak alone,
Strength is but a means to perdition.
It is wicked to seek greatness and glory,
Penury is sweeter than princedom.
Lightning does not threaten the corn-seed:
If the seed become a stack, it is unwise.
If you are sensible, you will be a mote of sand, not a Sahara,
So that you may enjoy the sunbeams.
O thou that delightest in the slaughter of sheep,
Slay thy self, and thou wilt have honour!
Life is rendered unstable
By violence, oppression, revenge, and exercise of power.

Though trodden underfoot, the grass grows up time after time
And washes the sleep of death from its eye again and again.
Forget thy self, if thou art wise!
If thou dost not forget thy self, thou art mad.
Close thine eyes, close thine ears, close thy lips,[1]
That thy thought may reach the lofty sky!
This pasturage of the world is naught, naught:
O fool, do not torment thyself for a phantom!"
The tiger-tribe was exhausted by hard struggles,
They had set their hearts on enjoyment of luxury.
This soporific advice pleased them,
In their stupidity they swallowed the charm of the sheep.

[1] Quoted from the *Masnavi*.

He that used to make sheep his prey
Now embraced a sheep's religion.
The tigers took kindly to a diet of fodder:
At length their tigerish nature was broken.
The fodder blunted their teeth
And put out the awful flashings of their eyes.
By degrees courage ebbed from their breasts,
The sheen departed from the mirror.
That frenzy of uttermost exertion remained not,
That craving after action dwelt in their hearts no more.
They lost the power of ruling and the resolution to be independent,
They lost reputation, prestige, and fortune.
Their paws that were as iron became strengthless;

Their souls died and their bodies became tombs.
Bodily strength diminished while spiritual fear increased:
Spiritual fear robbed them of courage.
Lack of courage produced a hundred diseases—
Poverty, pusillanimity, lowmindedness.
The wakeful tiger was lulled to slumber by the sheep's charm:
He called his decline Moral Culture.

VII

To the effect that Plato, whose thought has deeply influenced the mysticism and literature of Islam, followed the sheep's doctrine, and that we must be on our guard against his theories.[1]

PLATO, the prime ascetic and sage,
Was one of that ancient flock of sheep.

[1] The direct influence of Platonism on Moslem thought has been comparatively slight. When the Moslems began to study Greek philosophy, they turned to Aristotle. The genuine writings of Aristotle, however, were not accessible to them. They studied translations of books passing under his name, which were the work of Neoplatonists, so that what they believed to be Aristotelian doctrine was in fact the philosophy of Plotinus, Proclus, and the later Neoplatonic school. Indirectly, therefore, Plato has profoundly influenced the intellectual and spiritual development of Islam and may be called, if not the father of Mohammedan mysticism, at any rate its presiding genius.

His Pegasus went astray in the darkness of philosophy
And galloped over the mountains of Being.
He was so fascinated by the Ideal
That he made head, eye, and ear of no account.
"To die," said he, "is the secret of Life:
The candle is glorified by being put out."
He dominates our thinking,
His cup sends us to sleep and takes the world away from us.
He is a sheep in man's clothing,
The soul of the Súfí bows to his authority.
He soared with his intellect to the highest heaven,
He called the world of phenomena a myth.
'Twas his work to dissolve the structure of Life

And cut the bough of Life's fair tree asunder.
The thought of Plato regarded loss as profit,
His philosophy declared that being is not-being.
His nature drowsed and created a dream,
His mind's eye created a mirage.
Since he was without any taste for action,
His soul was enraptured by the non-existent.
He disbelieved in the material universe
And became the creator of invisible Ideas.
Sweet is the world of phenomena to the living spirit,
Dear is the world of Ideas to the dead spirit:
Its gazelles have no grace of movement,
Its partridges are denied the pleasure of walking daintily.

Its dewdrops are unable to quiver,
Its birds have no breath in their breasts,
Its seed does not desire to grow,
Its moths do not know how to flutter.
Our philosopher had no remedy but flight:
He could not endure the noise of this world.
He set his heart on the glow of a quenched flame
And depicted a world steeped in opium.
He spread his wings towards the sky
And never came down to his nest again.
His phantasy is sunk in the jar of heaven:
I know not whether it is the dregs or the bricks.[1]
The peoples were poisoned by his intoxication:
He slumbered and took no delight in deeds.

[1] *I.e.* it is worthless in either case. The egg-shaped wine-jar is supported by bricks in order to keep it in an upright position.

VIII

Concerning the true nature of poetry and the reform of Islamic literature.

'Tis the brand of desire makes the blood of man run warm,
By the lamp of desire this dust is enkindled.
By desire Life's cup is brimmed with wine,
So that Life leaps to its feet and marches briskly on.
Life is occupied with conquest alone,
And the one charm for conquest is desire.
Life is the hunter and desire the snare,
Desire is Love's message to Beauty.
Wherefore doth desire swell continuously

The bass and treble of Life's song?
Whatsoever is good and fair and beautiful
Is our guide in the wilderness of seeking.
Its image becomes impressed on thine heart,
It creates desires in thine heart.
Beauty is the creator of desire's spring-tide,
Desire is nourished by the display of Beauty.
'Tis in the poet's breast that Beauty unveils,
'Tis from his Sinai that Beauty's beams arise.
By his look the fair is made fairer,
Through his enchantments Nature is more beloved.
From his lips the nightingale hath learned her song,
And his rouge hath brightened the cheek of the rose.

'Tis his passion burns in the heart of the moth,
'Tis he that lends glowing hues to love-tales.
Sea and land are hidden within his water and clay,[1]
A hundred new worlds are concealed in his heart.
Ere tulips blossomed in his brain
There was heard no note of joy or grief.
His music breathes o'er us a wonderful enchantment,
His pen draws a mountain with a single hair.
His thoughts dwell with the moon and the stars,
He creates beauty in that which is ugly and strange.
He is a Khizr, and amidst his darkness is the Fountain of Life:[2]

[1] *I.e.* in his body.

[2] Khizr, according to the legend, discovered the Fountain of Life in the Land of Darkness.

All things that exist are made more living by his tears.
Heavily we go, like raw novices,
Stumbling on the way to the goal.
His nightingale hath played a tune
And laid a plot to beguile us,
That he may lead us into Life's Paradise,
And that Life's bow may become a full circle.
Caravans march at the sound of his bell
And follow the voice of his pipe;
But when his zephyr blows in our gardens,
We stay loitering amongst tulips and roses.
His witchery makes Life develop itself
And become self-questioning and impatient.
He invites the whole world to his table;
He lavishes his fire as though it were cheap as air.
Woe to a people that resigns itself to death,

And whose poet turns away from the
joy of living!
His mirror shows beauty as ugliness,
His honey leaves a hundred stings in
the heart.
His kiss robs the rose of freshness,
He takes away from the nightingale's
heart the joy of flying.
Thy sinews are relaxed by his opium,
Thou payest for his song with thy
life.
He bereaves the cypress of delight in
its beauty,
His cold breath makes a pheasant of
the male falcon.
He is a fish, and from the breast upward
a man,
Like the Sirens in the ocean.
With his song he enchants the pilot
And casts the ship to the bottom of
the sea.
His melodies steal firmness from thine
heart,

His magic persuades thee that death is life.
He takes from thy soul the desire of existence,
He extracts from thy mine the blushing ruby.
He dresses gain in the garb of loss,
He makes everything praiseworthy blameful.
He plunges thee in a sea of thought,
He makes thee a stranger to action.
He is sick, and by his words our sickness is increased:
The more his cup goes round, the more sick are they that quaff it.
There are no lightning-rains in his April,
His garden is a mirage of colour and perfume.
His beauty hath no dealings with Truth,
There are none but flawed pearls in his sea.
Slumber he deemed sweeter than waking:

Our fire was quenched by his breath.
By the chant of his nightingale the heart was poisoned:
Under his heap of roses lurked a snake.
Beware of his decanter and cup!
Beware of his sparkling wine!
O thou whom his wine hath laid low
And who look'st to his glass for thy rising dawn,
O thou whose heart hath been chilled by his melodies,
Thou hast drunk deadly poison through the ear!
Thy way of life is a proof of thy degeneracy,
The strings of thine instrument are out of tune.
'Tis pampered ease hath made thee so wretched,
A disgrace to Islam throughout the world.
One can bind thee with the vein of a rose,

One can wound thee with a zephyr.
Love hath been put to shame by thy wailing,
His fair picture hath been fouled by thy brush.
Thy ill-usage hath paled his cheek,
Thy coldness hath taken the glow from his fire.
He is heartsick from thy heart-sicknesses,
And enfeebled by thy feeblenesses.
His cup is full of childish tears,
His house is furnished with distressful sighs.[1]
He is a drunkard begging at tavern-doors,
Stealing glimpses of beauty from lattices,
Unhappy, melancholy, injured,
Kicked well-nigh to death by the warder;

[1] In this passage the author assails the Persian and Urdu poetry so much in favour with his contemporaries.

Wasted like a reed by sorrows,
On his lips a store of complaints against Heaven.
Flattery and spite are the mettle of his mirror,
Helplessness his comrade of old;
A miserable base-born underling
Without worth or hope or object,
Whose lamentations have sucked the marrow from thy soul
And driven off gentle sleep from thy neighbours' eyes.
Alas for a love whose fire is extinct,
A love that was born in the Holy Place and died in the house of idols!
Oh, if thou hast the coin of poesy in thy purse,
Rub it on the touchstone of Life!
Clear-seeing thought shows the way to action,
As the lightning-flash precedes the thunder.

It behoves thee to meditate well concerning literature,
It behoves thee to go back to the Arabs:
Thou must needs give thine heart to the Salmá of Araby,[1]
That the morn of the Hijáz may blossom from the night of Kurdistan.[2]
Thou hast gathered roses from the garden of Persia
And seen the springtide of India and Iran:

[1] Arabic odes usually begin with a prelude in which the poet makes mention of his beloved; and her name is often Salmá. Here "the Salmá of Araby" refers to the Koran and the ideals for which it stands.

[2] It is related that an ignorant Kurd came to some students and besought them to instruct him in the mysteries of Súfism. They told him that he must fasten a rope to the roof of his house, then tie the loose end to his feet and suspend himself, head downwards; and that he must remain in this posture as long as possible, reciting continually some words of gibberish which they taught him. The poor man did not perceive that he was being mocked. He followed their instructions and passed the whole night repeating the words given him. God rewarded his faith and sincerity by granting him illumination, so that he became a saint and could discourse learnedly on the most abstruse matters of mystical theology. Afterwards he used to say, "In the evening I was a Kurd, but the next morning I was an Arab."

Now taste a little of the heat of the desert,
Drink the old wine of the date!
Lay thine head for once on its hot breast,
Yield thy body awhile to its scorching wind!
For a long time thou hast turned about on a bed of silk:
Now accustom thyself to rough cotton!
For generations thou hast danced on tulips
And bathed thy cheek in dew, like the rose:
Now throw thyself on the burning sand
And plunge into the fountain of Zemzem!
How long wilt thou fain lament like the nightingale?
How long make thine abode in gardens?
O thou whose auspicious snare would do honour to the Phœnix,
Build a nest on the high mountains,

A nest embosomed in lightning and
thunder,
Loftier than eagle's eyrie,
That thou mayst be fit for Life's battle,
That thy body and soul may burn in
Life's fire!

IX

Showing that the education of the Self has three stages: Obedience, Self-control, and Divine Vicegerency.

1. Obedience

SERVICE and toil are traits of the camel,
Patience and perseverance are ways of the camel.
Noiselessly he steps along the sandy track,
He is the ship of those who voyage in the desert.
Every thicket knows the print of his foot:
He eats seldom, sleeps little, and is inured to toil.

He carries rider, baggage, and litter;
He trots on and on to the journey's end,
Rejoicing in his speed,
More patient in travel than his rider.
Thou, too, do not refuse the burden of Duty:
So wilt thou enjoy the best dwelling-place, which is with God.
Endeavour to obey, O heedless one!
Liberty is the fruit of compulsion.
By obedience the man of no worth is made worthy;
By disobedience his fire is turned to ashes.
Whoso would master the sun and stars,
Let him make himself a prisoner of Law!
The wind is enthralled by the fragrant rose;
The perfume is confined in the navel of the musk-deer.
The star moves towards its goal
With head bowed in surrender to a law.

The grass springs up in obedience to the law of growth:
When it abandons that, it is trodden underfoot.
To burn unceasingly is the law of the tulip,
And so the blood leaps in its veins.
Drops of water become a sea by the law of union,
And grains of sand become a Sahara.
Since Law makes everything strong within,
Why dost thou neglect this source of strength?
O thou that art emancipated from the old Custom,[1]
Adorn thy feet once more with the same fine silver chain!
Do not complain of the hardness of the Law,
Do not transgress the statutes of Mohammed!

[1] The religious law of Islam.

2. Self-control

Thy soul cares only for itself, like the camel:
It is self-conceited, self-governed, and self-willed.
Be a man, get its halter into thine hand,
That thou mayst become a pearl albeit thou art a potter's vessel.
He that does not command himself
Becomes a receiver of commands from others.
When they moulded thee of clay,
Love and fear were mingled in thy making:
Fear of this world and of the world to come, fear of death,
Fear of all the pains of earth and heaven;
Love of riches and power, love of country,
Love of self and kindred and wife.

The mixing of clay with water nourishes the body,[1]
But he that is drowned in sin dies an evil death.
So long as thou hold'st the staff of "There is no God but He,"[2]
Thou wilt break every spell of fear.
One to whom God is as the soul in his body,
His neck is not bowed before vanity.
Fear finds no way into his bosom,
His heart is afraid of none but Allah.
Whoso dwells in the Moslem Faith
Is free from the bonds of wife and child.
He withdraws his gaze from all except God
And lays the knife to the throat of his son.[3]

[1] *I.e.* water is an indispensable element in the life of the body.

[2] The first article of the Mohammedan creed.

[3] Like Abraham when he was about to sacrifice Isaac or (as Moslems generally believe) Ishmael.

Though single, he is like a host in onset:
Life is cheaper in his eyes than wind.
The profession of Faith is the shell, but prayer is the pearl:
The Moslem's heart deems prayer a lesser pilgrimage.[1]
In the Moslem's hand prayer is like a dagger
Killing sin and frowardness and wrong.
Fasting makes an assault upon hunger and thirst
And breaches the citadel of sensuality.
The pilgrimage enlightens the minds of the Faithful:
It teaches separation from one's home and destroys attachment to one's native land;
It is an act of devotion in which all feel themselves to be one,
It binds together the leaves of the book of religion.

[1] The lesser pilgrimage (*'umra*) is not obligatory like the greater pilgrimage (*hajj*).

Almsgiving causes love of riches to pass away
And makes equality familiar;
It fortifies the heart with righteousness,[1]
It increases wealth and diminishes fondness for wealth.
All this is a means of strengthening thee:
Thou art impregnable, if thy Islam be strong.
Draw might from the litany "O Almighty One!"
That thou mayst ride the camel of thy body.[2]

3. Divine Vicegerency[3]

If thou canst rule thy camel, thou wilt rule the world

[1] The original quotes part of a verse in the Koran (ch. 3, v. 86), where it is said, "Ye shall never attain unto righteousness until ye give in alms of that which ye love."

[2] *I.e.* overcome the lusts of the flesh.

[3] Here Iqbal interprets in his own way the Súfí doctrine of the *Insán al-kámil* or Perfect Man, which

And wear on thine head the crown of Solomon.
Thou wilt be the glory of the world whilst the world lasts,
And thou wilt reign in the kingdom incorruptible.
'Tis sweet to be God's vicegerent in the world
And exercise sway over the elements.
God's vicegerent is as the soul of the universe,
His being is the shadow of the Greatest Name.
He knows the mysteries of part and whole,
He executes the command of Allah in the world.
When he pitches his tent in the wide world,

---

teaches that every man is potentially a microcosm, and that when he has become spiritually perfect, all the Divine attributes are displayed by him, so that as saint or prophet he is the God-man, the representative and vicegerent of God on earth.

He rolls up this ancient carpet.[1]
His genius abounds with life and desires to manifest itself:
He will bring another world into existence.
A hundred worlds like this world of parts and wholes
Spring up, like roses, from the seed of his imagination.
He makes every raw nature ripe,
He puts the idols out of the sanctuary.
Heart-strings give forth music at his touch,
He wakes and sleeps for God alone.
He teaches age the melody of youth
And endows everything with the radiance of youth.
To the human race he brings both a glad message and a warning,
He comes both as a soldier and as a marshal and prince.

[1] *I.e.* his appearance marks the end of an epoch.

He is the final cause of "God taught Adam the names of all things,"[1]
He is the inmost sense of "Glory to Him that transported His servant by night."[2]
His white hand is strengthened by the staff,[3]
His knowledge is twinned with the power of a perfect man.
When that bold cavalier seizes the reins,
The steed of Time gallops faster.
His awful mien makes the Red Sea dry,
He leads Israel out of Egypt.
At his cry, "Arise," the dead spirits
Rise in their bodily tomb, like pines in the field.
His person is an atonement for all the world,

[1] Koran, ch. 2, v. 29. The Ideal Man is the final cause of creation.

[2] Koran, ch. 17, v. 1, referring to the Ascension of the Prophet.

[3] For the white hand (of Moses) cf. Koran, ch. 7, v. 105, ch. 26, v. 32, and Exodus, ch. 4, v. 6.

By his grandeur the world is saved.[1]
His protecting shadow makes the mote familiar with the sun,
His rich substance makes precious all that exists.
He bestows life by miraculous works,
He founds a new system to work by.
Splendid visions rise from the print of his foot,
Many a Moses is entranced by his Sinai.
He gives a new explanation of Life,
A new interpretation of this dream.
His hidden being is Life's mystery,
The unheard music of Life's harp.
Nature travails in blood for generations
To compose the harmony of his personality.
When our handful of earth has reached the zenith,

[1] These four lines may allude to Jesus, regarded as a type of the Perfect Man.

That champion will come forth from this dust!
There sleeps amidst the ashes of To-day
The flame of a world-consuming morrow.
Our bud enfolds a garden of roses,
Our eyes are bright with to-morrow's dawn.
Appear, O rider of Destiny!
Appear, O light of the dark realm of Change!
Illumine the scene of existence,
Dwell in the blackness of our eyes!
Silence the noise of the nations,
Imparadise our ears with thy music!
Arise and tune the harp of brotherhood,
Give us back the cup of the wine of love!
Bring once more days of peace to the world,
Give a message of peace to them that seek battle!

Mankind are the cornfield and thou the harvest,
Thou art the goal of Life's caravan.
The leaves are scattered by Autumn's fury:
Oh, do thou pass over our gardens as the Spring!
Receive from our downcast brows
The homage of little children and of young men and old!
When thou art there, we will lift up our heads,
Content to suffer the burning fire of this world.

X

Setting forth the inner meanings of the names of Ali.

ALI is the first Moslem and the King of men,
In Love's eyes Ali is the treasure of the Faith.
Devotion to his family inspires me with life
So that I am as a shining pearl.
Like the narcissus, I am enraptured with gazing;
Like perfume, I am straying through his pleasure-garden.
If holy water gushes from my earth, he is the source;

If wine pours from my grapes, he is the cause.
I am dust, but his sun hath made me as a mirror:
Song can be seen in my breast.
From Ali's face the Prophet drew a fair omen,
By his majesty the true religion is glorified.
His commandments are the strength of Islam:
All things pay allegiance to his House.
The Apostle of God gave him the name Bú Turáb;
God in the Koran called him "the Hand of Allah."
Every one that is acquainted with Life's mysteries
Knows what is the inner meaning of the names of Ali.
The dark clay, whose name is the body—
Our reason is ever bemoaning its iniquity.

On account of it our sky-reaching thought plods o'er the earth;
It makes our eyes blind and our ears deaf.
It hath in its hand a two-edged sword of lust:
Travellers' hearts are broken by this brigand.
Ali, the Lion of God, subdued the body's clay
And transmuted this dark earth to gold.
Murtazá, by whose sword the splendour of Truth was revealed,
Is named Bú Turáb from his conquest of the body.[1]
Man wins territory by prowess in battle,
But his brightest jewel is mastery of himself.
Whosoever in the world becomes a Bú Turáb
Turns back the sun from the west;[2]

[1] Murtazá, "he whom with God is pleased," is a name of Ali. Bú Turáb means literally "father of earth."

[2] A miracle of the Prophet.

Whosoever saddles tightly the steed of the body
Sits like the bezel on the seal of sovereignty:
Here the might of Khaibar is under his feet,[1]
And hereafter his hand will distribute the water of Kauthar.[2]
Through self-knowledge he acts as God's Hand,
And in virtue of being God's Hand he reigns over all.
His person is the gate of the city of the sciences:
Arabia, China, and Greece are subject to him.
If thou wouldst drink clear wine from thine own grapes,
Thou must needs wield authority over thine own earth.

[1] The fortress of Khaibar, a village in the Hijáz, was captured by the Moslems in A.D. 628. Ali performed great feats of valour on this occasion.

[2] A river of Paradise.

To become earth is the creed of a moth;
Be a conqueror of earth; that alone is worthy of a man.
Thou art soft as a rose. Become hard as a stone,
That thou mayst be the foundation of the wall of the garden!
Build thy clay into a Man,
Build thy Man into a World!
If thou art unfit to be either a wall or a door,
Some one else will make bricks of thine earth.
O thou who complainest of the cruelty of Heaven,
Thou whose glass cries out against the injustice of the stone,
How long this wailing and crying and lamentation?
How long this perpetual beating of thy breast?
The pith of Life is contained in action,
To delight in creation is the law of Life.

Arise and create a new world!
Wrap thyself in flames, be an Abraham![1]
To comply with this ill-starred world
Is to fling away thy buckler on the field of battle.
The man of strong character who is master of himself
Will find Fortune complaisant.
If the world does not comply with his humour,
He will try the hazard of war with Heaven;
He will dig up the foundations of the universe
And cast its atoms into a new mould.
He will subvert the course of Time
And wreck the azure firmament.
By his own strength he will produce
A new world which will do his pleasure.
If one cannot live in the world as beseems a man,

[1] See note on l. 213.

It is true life to give up one's soul.
He that hath sound intelligence
Will prove his strength by great enterprises.
'Tis sweet to use love in hard tasks
And, like Abraham, to gather roses from flames.[1]
The potentialities of men of action
Are displayed in willing acceptance of what is difficult.
Mean spirits have no weapon but spite,
This is their one rule of life.
But Life is power made manifest,
And its mainspring is the desire for victory.
Mercy out of season is a coldness of Life's blood,
A break in the rhythm of Life's music.
Whoever is sunk in the depths of ignominy
Calls his weakness contentment.

[1] The burning pyre on which Abraham was thrown lost its heat and was transformed into a rose-garden.

Weakness is the plunderer of Life,
Its womb is teeming with fears and lies.
Its soul is empty of virtues,
Its milk is a fattening for vices.
O man of sound judgement, beware!
This spoiler is lurking in ambush.
Be not his dupe, if thou art wise:
Chameleon-like, he changes colour every moment.
Even by keen observers his form is not discerned:
Veils are thrown over his face.
Now he is muffled in pity and gentleness,
Now he wears the cloak of humility.
Sometimes he is disguised as a victim of oppression,
Sometimes as one whose sins are to be excused.
He appears in the shape of self-indulgence
And robs the strong man's heart of courage.

Strength is the twin of Truth;
If thou knowest thyself, strength is the Truth-revealing glass.
Life is the seed, and power the crop:
Power explains the mystery of truth and falsehood.
The false claimant, if he be possessed of power,
Needs no argument for his claim.
Falsehood derives from power the authority of truth,
And by falsifying truth deems itself true.
Its creative word transforms poison into nectar;
It says to Good, "Thou art bad," and Good becomes Evil.
O thou that art heedless of the trust committed to thee,
Esteem thyself superior to both worlds![1]

[1] The "trust" which God offered to Man and which Man accepted, after it had been refused by Heaven and Earth (Koran, ch. 33, v. 72), is the divine vicegerency, *i.e.* the duty of displaying the divine attributes.

Gain knowledge of Life's mysteries!
Be a tyrant! Ignore all except God!
O man of understanding, open thine eyes, ears, and lips![1]
If then thou seest not the Way of Truth, laugh at me!

[1] A parody of the verse in the *Masnavi* quoted above. See l. 603.

XI

Story of a young man of Merv who came to the saint Ali Hujwírí—God have mercy on him!—and complained that he was oppressed by his enemies.

THE saint of Hujwír was venerated by the peoples,
And Pír-i Sanjar visited his tomb as a pilgrim.[1]
With ease he broke down the mountain-barriers
And sowed the seed of Islam in India.
The age of Omar was restored by his godliness,

[1] Hujwírí, author of the oldest Persian treatise on Súfism, was a native of Ghazna in Afghanistan. He died at Lahore about A.D. 1072. Pír-i Sanjar is the renowned saint, Mu'ínuddín, head of the Chishtí order of dervishes, who died in A.D. 1235 at Ajmír.

The fame of the Truth was exalted by his words.
He was a guardian of the honour of the Koran,
The house of Falsehood fell in ruins at his gaze.
The dust of the Panjáb was brought to life by his breath,
Our dawn was made splendid by his sun.
He was a lover, and withal a courier of Love:
The secrets of Love shone forth from his brow.
I will tell a story of his perfection
And enclose a whole rose-bed in a single bud.
A young man, cypress-tall,
Came from the town of Merv to Lahore.
He went to see the venerable saint,
That the sun might dispel his darkness.
"I am hemmed in," he said, "by foes;
I am as a glass in the midst of stones.

Do thou teach me, O sire of heavenly rank,
How to lead my life amongst enemies!"
The wise Director, in whose nature
Love had allied mercy with wrath,
Answered: "Thou art unread in Life's lore,
Careless of its end and its beginning.
Be without fear of others!
Thou art a sleeping force: awake!
When the stone was anxious on account of the glass,
It became glass and got into the way of breaking.
If the traveller thinks himself weak,
He delivers his soul unto the brigand.
How long wilt thou regard thyself as water and clay?
Create from thy clay a flaming Sinai!
Why be angry with mighty men?
Why complain of enemies?
I will declare the truth: thine enemy is thy friend;

His existence crowns thee with glory.
Whosoever knows the states of the Self
Considers a powerful enemy to be a blessing from God.
To the seed of Man the enemy is as a rain-cloud:
He awakens its potentialities.
If thy spirit be strong, the stones in thy way are as water:
What recks the torrent of the ups and downs of the road?
The sword of resolution is whetted by the stones in the way
And put to proof by traversing stage after stage.
What is the use of eating and sleeping like a beast?
What is the use of being, unless thou have strength in thyself?
When thou mak'st thyself strong with Self,
Thou wilt destroy the world at thy pleasure.

If thou wouldst pass away, become free
of Self;
If thou wouldst live, become full of
Self![1]
What is death? To become oblivious
to Self.
Why imagine that it is the parting of
soul and body?
Abide in Self, like Joseph!
Advance from captivity to empire!
Think of Self and be a man of action!
Be a man of God, bear mysteries
within!"

I will explain the matter by means of
stories,
I will open the bud by the power of
my breath.
"'Tis better that a lovers' secret
Should be told by the lips of others."[2]

[1] These lines correct the Súfí doctrine that by means of passing away from individuality the mystic attains to everlasting life in God.

[2] *I.e.* allegorically. This verse occurs in the *Masnavi*.

XII

Story of the bird that was faint with thirst.

A BIRD was faint with thirst,
The breath in his body was heaving like waves of smoke.
He saw a diamond in the garden :
Thirst created a vision of water.
Deceived by the sunbright stone
The foolish bird fancied that it was water.
He got no moisture from the gem :
He pecked it with his beak, but it did not wet his palate.
"O thrall of vain desire," said the diamond,

"Thou hast sharpened thy greedy beak on me;
But I am not a dewdrop, I give no drink,
I do not live for the sake of others.
Wouldst thou hurt me? Thou art mad!
A life that reveals the Self is strange to thee.
My water will shiver the beaks of birds
And break the jewel of man's life."[1]
The bird won not his heart's wish from the diamond
And turned away from the sparkling stone.
Disappointment swelled in his breast,
The song in his throat became a wail.
Upon a rose-twig a drop of dew
Gleamed like the tear in a nightingale's eye:
All its glitter was owing to the sun,
It was trembling in fear of the sun—

[1] *I.e.* if he swallow a diamond, he will die.

A restless sky-born star
That had stopped for a moment, from desire to be seen;
Oft deceived by bud and flower,
It had gained nothing from Life.
There it hung, ready to drop,
Like a tear on the eyelashes of a lover who hath lost his heart.
The sorely distressed bird hopped under the rose-bush,
The dewdrop trickled into his mouth.
O thou that wouldst deliver thy soul from enemies,
I ask thee—"Art thou a drop of water or a gem?"
When the bird melted in the fire of thirst,
It appropriated the life of another.
The drop was not solid and gem-like;
The diamond had a being, the drop had none.
Never for an instant neglect Self-preservation:

Be a diamond, not a dewdrop!
Be massive in nature, like mountains,
And bear on thy crest a hundred clouds laden with floods of rain!
Save thyself by affirmation of Self,
Compress thy quicksilver into silver ore!
Produce a melody from the string of Self,
Make manifest the secrets of Self!

XIII

Story of the diamond and the coal.

Now I will open one more gate of Truth,
I will tell thee another tale.
The coal in the mine said to the diamond,
"O thou entrusted with splendours everlasting,
We are comrades, and our being is one;
The source of our existence is the same,
Yet while I die here in the anguish of worthlessness,
Thou art set on the crowns of emperors.

My stuff is so vile that I am valued less than earth,
Whereas the mirror's heart is rent by thy beauty.
My darkness illumines the chafing-dish,
Then my substance is incinerated at last.
Every one puts the sole of his foot on my head
And covers my stock of existence with ashes.
My fate must needs be deplored;
Dost thou know what is the gist of my being?
Thou art a condensed wavelet of smoke,
Endowed with the properties of a single spark;
Both in feature and nature thou art star-like,
Splendours rise from every side of thee.
Now thou becom'st the light of a monarch's eye,

Now thou adornest the haft of a dagger."
"O sagacious friend!" said the diamond,
"Dark earth, when hardened, becomes in dignity as a bezel.
Having been at strife with its environment,
It is ripened by the struggle and grows hard like a stone.
'Tis this ripeness that has endowed my form with light
And filled my bosom with radiance.
Because thy being is immature, thou hast become abased;
Because thy body is soft, thou art burnt.
Be void of fear, grief, and anxiety;
Be hard as a stone, be a diamond!
Whosoever strives hard and grips tight,
The two worlds are illumined by him.
A little earth is the origin of the Black Stone

Which puts forth its head in the Ka'ba:
Its rank is higher than Sinai,
It is kissed by the swarthy and the fair.
In solidity consists the glory of Life;
Weakness is worthlessness and immaturity."

XIV

Story of the Sheikh and the Brahmin, followed by a conversation between Ganges and Himalaya to the effect that the continuation of social life depends on firm attachment to the characteristic traditions of the community.

At Benares lived a venerable Brahmin,
Whose head was deep in the ocean of
 Being and Not-being.
He had a large knowledge of philosophy
But was well-disposed to the seekers
 after God.
His mind was eager to explore new
 problems,
His intellect moved on a level with the
 Pleiades;

His nest was as high as that of the Anká;[1]
Sun and moon were cast, like rue, on the flame of his thought.[2]
For a long time he laboured and sweated,
But philosophy brought no wine to his cup.
Although he set many a snare in the gardens of learning,
His snares never caught a glimpse of the Ideal bird;
And notwithstanding that the nails of his thought were dabbled with blood,
The knot of Being and Not-being remained untied.
The sighs on his lips bore witness to his despair,
His countenance told tales of his distraction.
One day he visited an excellent Sheikh,

[1] A mysterious bird, of which nothing is known except its name.

[2] Rue-seed is burned for the purpose of fumigation.

A man who had in his breast a heart of gold.
The Sheikh laid the seal of silence on his lips
While he lent his ear to the Sage's discourse.
Then he said: "O wanderer in the lofty sky,
Pledge thyself to be true, for a little, to the earth!
Thou hast lost thy way in wildernesses of speculation,
Thy fearless thought hath passed beyond Heaven.
Be reconciled with earth, O sky-traveller!
Do not wander in quest of the essence of the stars!
I do not bid thee abandon thine idols.
Art thou an unbeliever? Then be worthy of the badge of unbelief![1]

[1] "The badge of unbelief": here the original has *zunnár* (ζωνάριον), *i.e.* the sacred thread worn by Zoroastrians and other non-Moslems.

O inheritor of ancient culture,
Turn not thy back on the path thy fathers trod!
If a people's life is derived from unity,
Unbelief too is a source of unity.
Thou that art not even a perfect infidel
Art unfit to worship at the shrine of the spirit.
We both are far astray from the road of devotion:
Thou art far from Ázar, and I from Abraham.[1]
Our Majnún hath not fallen into melancholy for his Lailá's sake:
He hath not become perfect in the madness of love.
When the lamp of Self expires,
What is the use of heaven-surveying imagination?"

Once on a time, laying hold of the skirt of the mountain,

[1] Ázar, the father of Abraham, was an idolater.

Ganges said to Himalaya:
"O thou mantled in snow since the morn of creation,
Thou whose form is girdled with streams,
God made thee a partner in the secrets of heaven,
But deprived thy foot of graceful gait.
He took away from thee the power to walk:
What avails this sublimity and stateliness?
Life springs from perpetual movement:
Motion constitutes the wave's whole existence."
When the mountain heard this taunt from the river,
He puffed angrily like a sea of fire,
And answered: "Thy wide waters are my looking-glass;
Within my bosom are a hundred rivers like thee.

This graceful gait of thine is an instrument of death:
Whoso goeth from Self is meet to die.
Thou hast no knowledge of thine own case,
Thou exultest in thy misfortune: thou art a fool!
O born of the womb of the revolving sphere,
A fallen-in bank is better than thou!
Thou hast made thine existence an offering to the ocean,
Thou hast thrown the rich purse of thy life to the highwayman.
Be self-contained like the rose in the garden,
Do not go to the florist in order to smell sweet!
To live is to grow in thyself
And gather roses from thine own flower-bed.
Ages have gone by and my foot is fast in earth:

Dost thou fancy that I am far from my goal?
My being grew and reached the sky,
The Pleiads sank to rest under my skirts;
Thy being vanishes in the ocean,
But on my crest the stars bow their heads.
Mine eye sees the mysteries of heaven,
Mine ear is familiar with angels' wings.
Since I glowed with the heat of unceasing toil,
I amassed rubies, diamonds, and other gems.
I am stone within, and in the stone is fire:
Water cannot pass over my fire!"
Art thou a drop of water? Do not break at thine own feet,
But endeavour to surge and wrestle with the sea.
Desire the water of a jewel, become a jewel!

Be an ear-drop, adorn a beauty!
Oh, expand thyself! Move swiftly!
Be a cloud that shoots lightning and sheds a flood of rain!
Let the ocean sue for thy storms as a beggar,
Let it complain of the straitness of thy skirts!
Let it deem itself less than a wave
And glide along at thy feet!

XV

Showing that the purpose of the Moslem's life is to exalt the Word of Allah, and that the Jihád (war against unbelievers), if it be prompted by land-hunger, is unlawful in the religion of Islam.

Imbue thine heart with the tincture of Allah,
Give honour and glory to Love!
The Moslem's nature prevails by means of love:
The Moslem, if he be not loving, is an infidel.
Upon God depends his seeing and not-seeing,
His eating, drinking, and sleeping.

In his will that which God wills becomes lost—
"How shall a man believe this saying?"[1]
He encamps in the field of "There is no god but Allah";
In the world he is a witness against mankind.
His high estate is attested by the Prophet that was sent to men and Jinn—
By the most truthful of witnesses.
Leave words and seek that spiritual state,
Shed the light of God o'er the darkness of works!
Albeit clad in kingly robe, live as a dervish,
Live wakeful and meditating on God!
Whatever thou doest, let it be thine aim therein to draw nigh to God,
That His glory may be made manifest by thee.

[1] See Introduction, p. xix, note 1.

Peace becomes an evil, if its object be aught else;
War is good if its object is God.
If God be not exalted by our swords,
War dishonours the people.
The holy Sheikh Miyán Mír Walí,[1]
By the light of whose soul every hidden thing was revealed—
His feet were firmly planted on the path of Mohammed,
He was a flute for the impassioned music of love.
His tomb keeps our city safe from harm
And causes the beams of true religion to shine on us.
Heaven stooped its brow to his threshold,
The Emperor of India was one of his disciples.[2]
Now, this monarch had sown the seed of ambition in his heart
And was resolved on conquest.

[1] A celebrated Moslem saint, who died at Lahore in A.D. 1635.
[2] Aurangzíb.

The flames of vain desire were alight in him,
He was teaching his sword to ask, "Is there any more?"[1]
In the Deccan was a great noise of war,
His army stood on the battlefield.
He went to the Sheikh of heaven-high dignity
That he might receive his blessing:
The Moslem turns from this world to God
And strengthens policy with prayer.
The Sheikh made no answer to the Emperor's speech,
The assembly of dervishes was all ears,
Until a disciple, in his hand a silver coin,
Opened his lips and broke the silence,
Saying, "Accept this poor offering from me,
O guide of them that have lost the way to God!

[1] Koran, ch. 50, v. 29.

My limbs were bathed in sweat of labour
Before I put away a dirhem in my skirt."
The Sheikh said: "This money ought to be given to our Sultan,
Who is a beggar wearing the raiment of a king.
Though he holds sway over sun, moon, and stars,
Our Emperor is the most penniless of mankind.
His eye is fixed on the table of strangers,
The fire of his hunger hath consumed a whole world.
His sword is followed by famine and plague,
His culture lays a wide land waste.
The folk are crying out because of his indigence,
His empty-headedness, and his oppression of the weak.
His power is an enemy to all:

Humankind are the caravan and he the brigand.
In his self-delusion and ignorance
He calls pillage by the name of empire.
Both the royal troops and those of the enemy
Are cloven in twain by the sword of his hunger.
The beggar's hunger consumes his own soul,
But the sultan's hunger destroys state and religion.
Whoso shall draw the sword for anything except Allah,
His sword is sheathed in his own breast."

XVI

Precepts written for the Moslems of India by Mír Naját Nakshband, who is generally known as Bábá Sahrá'í.[1]

O THOU that hast grown from earth, like a rose,
Thou too art born of the womb of Self.
Do not abandon Self! Persist therein!
Be a drop of water and drink up the ocean!
Glowing with the light of Self as thou art,
Make Self strong, and thou wilt endure.

[1] This appears to be a pseudonym assumed by the author.

Thou gett'st profit from this trade,
Thou gain'st riches by preserving this commodity.
Thou hast being, and art thou afraid of not-being?
O foolish one, thy understanding is at fault.
Since I am acquainted with the harmony of Life,
I will tell thee what is the secret of Life—
To sink into thyself like the pearl,
Then to emerge from thine inward solitude;
To collect sparks beneath the ashes,
And become a flame and dazzle men's eyes.
Go, burn the house of forty years' tribulation,
Move round thyself! Be a circling flame!
What is Life but to be freed from moving round others

And to regard thyself as the Holy Temple?
Beat thy wings and escape from the attraction of Earth;
Like birds, be safe from falling.
Unless thou art a bird, thou wilt do wisely
Not to build thy nest on the top of a cave.
O thou that seekest to acquire knowledge,
I say o'er to thee the message of the Sage of Rúm:[1]
"Knowledge, if it lie on thy skin, is a snake;
Knowledge, if thou take it to heart, is a friend."
Hast thou heard how the Master of Rúm
Gave lectures on philosophy at Aleppo?—
Fast in the bonds of intellectual proofs,

[1] Jaláluddín Rúmí.

Drifting o'er the dark and stormy sea of understanding;
A Moses unillumined by Love's Sinai,
Ignorant of Love and of Love's passion.
He discoursed on Scepticism and Neoplatonism,
And strung many a brilliant pearl of metaphysic.
He unravelled the problems of the Peripatetics,
The light of his thought made clear whatever was obscure.
Heaps of books lay around and in front of him,
And on his lips was the key to all their mysteries.
Shams-i Tabríz, directed by Kamál,[1]
Sought his way to the college of Jaláluddín Rúmí
And cried out, "What is all this noise and babble?

[1] Bábá Kamáluddín Jundí. For Shams-i Tabríz and his relation to Jaláluddín Rúmí see my *Selected Poems from the Díváni Shamsi Tabríz* (Cambridge, 1898).

What are all these syllogisms and judgements and demonstrations?"
"Peace, O fool!" exclaimed the Maulavi,
"Do not laugh at the doctrines of the sages.
Get thee out of my college!
This is argument and discussion: what hast thou to do with it?
My discourse is beyond thy understanding,
It will not brighten the glass of thy perception."
These words increased the anger of Shams-i Tabríz
And caused a fire to burst forth from his soul.
The lightning of his look fell on the earth,
And the glow of his breath made the dust spring into flames.
The spiritual fire burned the intellectual stack

And clean consumed the book of philosophy.
The Maulavi, being a stranger to Love's miracles
And unversed in Love's harmonies,
Cried, "How didst thou kindle this fire,
Which hath burned the books of the philosophers?"
The Sheikh answered, "O unbelieving Moslem,
This is vision and ecstasy: what hast thou to do with it?
My state is beyond thy thought,
My flame is the Alchemist's elixir."
Thou hast drawn thy substance from the snow of philosophy,
The cloud of thy thought sheds nothing but hailstones.
Kindle a fire in thy rubble,
Foster a flame in thy earth!
The Moslem's knowledge is perfected by spiritual fervour,

The meaning of Islam is *Renounce what shall pass away.*
When Abraham escaped from the bondage of "that which sets,"[1]
He sat unhurt in the midst of flames.[2]
Thou hast cast knowledge of God behind thee
And squandered thy religion for the sake of a loaf.
Thou art hot in pursuit of antimony,
Thou art unaware of the blackness of thine own eye.
Seek the Fountain of Life from the sword's edge,
And the River of Paradise from the dragon's mouth,
Demand the Black Stone from the door of the house of idols,
And the musk-deer's bladder from a mad dog,

[1] Abraham refused to worship the sun, moon, and stars, saying, "I love not them that set" (Koran, ch. 6, v. 76).

[2] See p. 91, note.

But do not seek the glow of Love from the knowledge of to-day,
Do not seek the nature of Truth from this infidel's cup!
Long have I been running to and fro,
Learning the secrets of the New Knowledge:
Its gardeners have put me to the trial
And have made me intimate with their roses.
Roses! Tulips, rather, that warn one not to smell them—
Like paper roses, a mirage of perfume.
Since this garden ceased to enthral me,
I have nested on the Paradisal tree.
Modern knowledge is the greatest blind—
Idol-worshipping, idol-selling, idol-making!
Shackled in the prison of phenomena,
It has not overleaped the limits of the sensible.

It has fallen down in crossing the bridge of Life,
It has laid the knife to its own throat.
Having fire, it is yet cold as the tulip;
Having flame, it is yet cold as hail.
Its nature remains untouched by the glow of Love,
It is ever engaged in a joyless search.
Love is the Plato that heals the sicknesses of the mind:[1]
The mind's melancholy is cured by its lancet.
The whole world bows in adoration to Love,
Love is the Mahmúd that conquers the Somnath of intellect.[2]
Modern science lacks this old wine in its cup,
Its nights are not loud with passionate prayer.

[1] In the *Masnavi* Love is called "the physician of our pride and self-conceit, our Plato and our Galen."

[2] The famous idol of Somnath was destroyed by Sultan Mahmúd of Ghazna.

Thou hast misprized thine own cypress
And deemed tall the cypress of others.
Like the reed, thou hast emptied thyself of Self
And given thine heart to the music of others.
O thou that begg'st morsels from another's table,
Wilt thou seek thine own kind in another's shop?
The Moslem's feast is burned up by the lamps of strangers,
His mosque is consumed by the Christian monastery.
When the deer fled from the sacred territory of Mecca,
The hunter's arrow pierced her side.[1]
The leaves of the rose are scattered, like its scent:
O thou that hast fled from thy Self, come back to it!

[1] The pilgrims are forbidden to kill game.

O trustee of the wisdom of the Koran,
Find thy lost unity again!
We, who keep the gate of the citadel of Islam,
Have become unbelievers by neglecting the watchword of Islam.
The ancient Saki's bowl is shattered,
The wine-party of the Hijáz is broken up.
The Ka'ba is filled with our idols,
Infidelity mocks at our Islam.
Our Sheikh hath gambled Islam away for love of idols
And made a rosary of the *zunnár*.[1]
Our spiritual directors owe their rank to their white hairs
And are the laughing-stock of children in the street;
Their hearts bear no impress of the Faith
But house the idols of sensuality.

[1] See p. 110, note.

Every long-haired fellow wears the garb of a dervish—
Alas for these traffickers in religion!
Day and night they are travelling about with disciples,
And ignoring their religious duties.
Their eyes are without light, like the narcissus,
Their breasts devoid of spiritual wealth.
Preachers and Súfís, all worship worldliness alike;
The prestige of the pure religion is ruined.
Our preacher fixed his eyes on the pagoda
And the mufti of the Faith sold his decision.
After this, O friends, what are we to do?
Our guide turns his face towards the wine-house.

XVII

Time is a sword.

GREEN be the pure grave of Sháfi'í,[1]
Whose vine hath cheered a whole world!
His thought plucked a star from heaven:
He named Time "a cutting sword."
How shall I say what is the secret of this sword?
All its brilliance is derived from Life.
Its owner is exalted above hope and fear,
His hand is whiter than the hand of Moses.

[1] Founder of one of the four great Mohammedan schools of law.

At one stroke thereof water gushes from the rock
And the sea becomes land from dearth of moisture.
Moses held this sword in his hand,
Therefore he wrought more than man may contrive.
He clove the Red Sea asunder
And made its waters like dry earth.
The arm of Ali, the conqueror of Khaibar,
Drew its strength from this same sword.
The revolution of the sky is visible,
The change of day and night is perceived.
Look, O thou enthralled by Yesterday and To-morrow,
Behold another world in thine own heart!
Thou hast sown the seed of darkness in thy clay,
Thou hast imagined Time as a line:
Thy thought measures length of Time
With the measure of night and day.

Thou mak'st this line a girdle on thine infidel waist;
Thou art an advertiser of falsehood, like idols.
Thou wert the Elixir, and thou hast become a peck of dust;
Thou wert born the conscience of Truth, and thou hast become a lie!
Art thou a Moslem? Then cast off this girdle!
Be a candle to the feast of the religion of the free!
Knowing not the origin of Time,
Thou art ignorant of everlasting Life.
How long wilt thou be a thrall of night and day?
Learn the mystery of Time from the words "I have a time with God."[1]
Phenomena arise from the march of Time,

[1] The Prophet said, "I have a time with God of such sort that neither angel nor prophet is my peer," meaning (if we interpret his words according to the sense of this passage) that he felt himself to be timeless.

Life is a part of the contents of Time's consciousness.
The cause of Time is not the revolution of the sun:
Time is everlasting, but the sun does not last for ever.
Time is joy and sorrow, festival and fast;
Time is the secret of moonlight and sunlight.
Thou hast extended Time, like Space,
And distinguished Yesterday from To-morrow.
Thou hast fled, like a scent, from thine own garden;
Thou hast made thy prison with thine own hand.
Our Time, which has neither beginning nor end,
Blossoms from the flower-bed of our mind.
To know its root quickens the living with new life:

Its being is more splendid than the dawn.
Life is of Time, and Time is of Life:
"Do not abuse Time!" was the command of the Prophet.

Oh, the memory of those days when Time's sword
Was allied with the strength of our hands![1]
We sowed the seed of religion in men's hearts
And unveiled the face of Truth;
Our nails tore loose the knot of this world,
Our bowing in prayer gave blessings to the earth.
From the jar of Truth we made rosy wine gush forth,
We charged against the ancient taverns.
O thou in whose cup is old wine,

[1] The glorious days when Islam first set out to convert and conquer the world.

A wine so hot that the glass is well-nigh turned to water,
Wilt thou in thy pride and arrogance and self-conceit
Taunt us with our emptiness?
Our cup, too, hath graced the symposium;
Our breast hath owned a spirit.
A new age hath been endued with our beauty
And hath risen from the dust of our feet.
Our blood hath watered God's harvest,
All worshippers of God are our debtors.
The *takbír* was our gift to the world,[1]
Ka'bas were built of our clay.
By means of us God taught the Koran,
From our hand He dispensed His bounty.
Although crown and signet have passed from us,

[1] The *takbír* is the cry "*Allah akbar*," "Allah is most great."

Do not look with contempt on our beggarliness!
In thine eyes we are good for nothing,
Thinking old thoughts, despicable.
We have honour from "There is no god but Allah,"
We are the preservers of the universe.
Freed from the vexation of to-day and to-morrow,
We have pledged ourselves to love One.
We are the conscience hidden in God's heart,
We are the heirs of Moses and Aaron.
Sun and moon are still bright with our radiance,
Lightning-flashes still lurk in our cloud.
Our essence is the mirror of the Divine essence:
The Moslem's being is one of the signs of God.

XVIII

An invocation.

O Thou that art as the soul in the body of the universe,
Thou art our soul and thou art ever fleeing from us.
Thou breathest music into Life's lute;
Life envies Death when death is for thy sake.
Once more bring comfort to our sad hearts,
Once more dwell in our breasts!
Once more let us hear thy call to honour,
Strengthen our weak love.
We are oft complaining of destiny,

Thou art of great price and we have naught.
Hide not thy fair face from the empty-handed!
Sell cheap the love of Salmán and Bilál![1]
Give us the sleepless eye and the passionate heart,
Give us again the nature of quicksilver!
Show unto us one of thy manifest signs,
That the necks of our enemies may be bowed!
Make this chaff a mountain crested with fire,
Burn with our fire all that is not God!
When the people let the clue of Unity go from their hands,
They fell into a hundred mazes.
We are dispersed like stars in the world;
Though of the same family, we are strange to one another.

[1] Salmán was a Persian, Bilál an Abyssinian. Both had been slaves and were devoted henchmen of the Prophet.

Bind again these scattered leaves,
Revive the law of love!
Take us back to serve thee as of old,
Commit thy cause to them that love thee!
We are travellers: give us devotion as our goal!
Give us the strong faith of Abraham!
Make us know the meaning of "There is no god,"
Make us acquainted with the mystery of "except Allah"!
I who burn like a candle for the sake of others
Teach myself to weep like the candle.
O God! a tear that is heart-enkindling,
Passionful, wrung forth by pain, peace-consuming,
May I sow in the garden, and may it grow into a fire
That washes away the fire-brand from the tulip's robe!

My heart is with yestereve, my eye is on to-morrow:
Amidst the company I am alone.
"Every one fancies he is my friend,
But my secret thoughts have not escaped from my heart."
Oh, where in the wide world is my comrade?
I am the Bush of Sinai: where is my Moses?
I am tyrannous, I have done many a wrong to myself,
I have nourished a flame in my bosom,
A flame that seized the furniture of judgement,
And cast fire on the skirt of discretion,
And lessoned with madness the reason,
And burned up the existence of knowledge:
Its blaze enthrones the sun in the sky,
And lightnings encircle it with adoration for ever.
Mine eye fell to weeping, like dew,

Since I was entrusted with that hidden fire.
I taught the candle to burn openly,
While I myself burned unseen by the world's eye.
At last flames breathed from every hair of me,
Fire dropped from the veins of my thought:
My nightingale picked up the spark-grains
And created a fire-tempered song.
Is the breast of this age without a heart?
Majnún trembles lest Lailá's howdah be empty.
It is not easy for the candle to throb alone:
Ah, is there no moth worthy of me?
How long shall I wait for one to share my grief?
How long must I search for a confidant?

O Thou whose face lends light to the moon and the stars,
Withdraw thy fire from my soul!
Take back what Thou hast put in my breast,
Remove the stabbing radiance from my mirror,
Or give me one old comrade
To be the mirror of mine all-burning love!
In the sea wave tosses side by side with wave:
Each hath a partner in its emotion.
In heaven star consorts with star,
And the bright moon lays her head on the knees of Night.
Morning touches Night's dark side,
And To-day throws itself against To-morrow.
One river loses its being in another,
A waft of air dies in perfume.
There is dancing in every nook of the wine-house,
Madman dances with madman.

Howbeit in thine essence Thou art single,
Thou hast decked out for Thyself a whole world.
I am as the tulip of the field,
In the midst of a company I am alone.
I beg of Thy grace a sympathising friend,
An adept in the mysteries of my nature,
A friend endowed with madness and wisdom,
One that knoweth not the phantom of vain things,
That I may confide my lament to his soul
And see again my face in his heart.
His image I will mould of mine own clay,
I will be to him both idol and worshipper.

THE END